MEETING GOD BIBLE STUDIES

MEETING GOD IN FORGIVENESS

Stephen D. Eyre

6 studies for individuals or groups

D1548106

InterVarsity Press
Downers Grove, Illinois

FORGIVENESS

InterVarsity Press
P.O. Box 1400, Downers Grove, IL 60515
World Wide Web: www.ivpress.com
E-mail: mail@ivpress.com

InterVarsity Press® is the book-publishing division of InterVarsity Christian Fellowship/USA®, a student movement active on campus at hundreds of universities, colleges and schools of nursing in the United States of America, and a member movement of the International Fellowship of Evangelical Students. For information about local and regional activities, write Public Relations Dept., InterVarsity Christian Fellowship/USA, 6400 Schroeder Rd., P.O. Box 7895, Madison, WI 53707-7895.

Cover illustration: Roberta Polfus

ISBN 0-8308-2053-1

Printed in the United States of America ♾

15	14	13	12	11	10	9	8	7	6	5	4	3	2	1
10	09	08	07	06	05	04	03	02	01	00	99			

Contents

INTRODUCING   5

Meeting God in Forgiveness

1 THE CONSEQUENCES OF SIN   9

Practicing the Discipline of Scripture Study   *2 Samuel 12:1-25*

2 TURNING TO GOD WITH OUR SIN   13

Practicing the Discipline of Confession   *Psalm 51*

3 GUIDELINES FOR FORGIVING OTHERS   18

Practicing the Discipline of Community   *Matthew 18:15-20*

4 RECEIVING GOD'S FORGIVENESS   23

Practicing the Discipline of Silence   *1 Peter 3:8-9; Colossians 3:13-17*

5 WHEN YOU DON'T WANT TO FORGIVE   27

Practicing the Discipline of Obedience   *1 Samuel 24*

6 KEEPING PERSPECTIVE   32

Practicing the Discipline of Prayer   *Matthew 6:1-15*

Guidelines for Leaders   37

Study Notes   41

INTRODUCING
Meeting God in Forgiveness

You could cut the tension in the room with a knife. Bill was in charge of the facilities team and he didn't like the way the compassion ministry had left the dining room after feeding all those people. He had to spend several extra hours of his day finishing the job that should have been done by the volunteers. To make his point, he sent them a bill for his time.

Sharon and the compassion team were furious. They had given hours, days, of their time preparing for the holiday meal to feed several thousand needy people at our church. Instead of appreciation for their hard work, they were billed for what they didn't do to meet some housekeeping standard.

Instead of talking to each other, they talked about each other. Sharon circulated a memo and called a few people on the church board to make her feelings known. Bill came to me with a copy of the memo and explained in detail the things he had to do to put the kitchen in shape for the next group of people.

Now after a couple of months of behind-the-scenes wrangling, we were all in the room together. Over the next hours the feelings came out and frustrations were aired. Unexpressed frustration and unexpressed hurts had been building for years, some of which went back to the attitudes and actions of the staff that were no longer around.

As the feelings, anger and hurts were aired, the light began to dispel the shadows. Slowly the tension began to subside. About a hour into the meeting, Bill looked Sharon in the eye and asked forgiveness for not being more responsive and sensitive. About a half hour later, Sharon turned to face Bill and apologized for not understanding what additional burdens she had placed on his job. We are now ready to move on in a shared ministry of caring in service in ways that weren't possible before.

The Healing Power of Forgiveness

Forgiveness breaks the chains of the past and opens the door to new relational realities. But forgiveness heals people, not just relationships. A physician at a mental institution was overheard to say "Half the people in here could walk out today if they could believe that they were forgiven." A worker in the inner city dealing with the down-and-outers of our culture said in an interview that the heart of helping people was believing that they were forgivable.

Being able to forgive and to receive forgiveness are central dynamics of the Christian faith. John the Baptist prepared the nation of Israel for the coming of Jesus by offering forgiveness of sins (Luke 3:3). One of Jesus' first acts of healing involved offering forgiveness to the paralytic who was lowered through the roof, saying, "Son, your sins are forgiven" (Mark 2:5). When Peter continues the ministry of Jesus on the day of Pentecost, he offers the invitation, "Repent and be baptized . . . for the forgiveness of sins" (Acts 2:38). And apostle Paul instructs the early Christians on how to live together by writing, "Be kind and compassionate to one another, forgiving each other, just as in Christ God has forgiven you" (Ephesians 4:32).

Forgiveness is an act of the heart. You can tell yourself that you have been forgiven by God, but believing it in the depths of your heart, is something else. Likewise, you can determine to forgive another person, but freely forgiving from the heart is something altogether different.

The heart can't be managed or commanded. Just as you can't

command your heart to love, you can't command it to forgive. Just as we can increase the health of our physical hearts through diet and exercise, so we can increase the health of our spiritual health through spiritual diet and spiritual exercise. It is a spiritually healthy heart that bears the fruit of forgiveness.

To shift the image slightly, we can't manufacture forgiveness in our hearts, but we can grow it. We can cultivate a heart of forgiveness. If we keep the soil of our hearts fertilized with scriptural truth, if we keep in soft with prayer and worship, and if we quickly pull the weeds of bitterness and hostility, the forgiveness of God will grow in our hearts.

In this guide on forgiveness as a spiritual discipline, we will explore the dynamics of forgiveness and put into practice spiritual truths that soften our hearts and cultivate a disposition to forgive. Looking at David's sin with Bathsheba, we discover the first barrier to forgiveness is facing the blinders we have to admitting our sin. David's poetic lament in Psalm 51 reveals how forgiveness calls out for a sense of cleansing, not just a legal pronouncement. From Jesus' teaching we see that the experience of forgiveness means we must extend that forgiveness to others. Through the instructions of the apostles, we will spend time in worshipful prayer, asking God to work forgiveness deep into our hearts. Then we return to David, a young warrior who knew that forgiveness, not vengeance, was to be the true foundation of a kingdom. Finally, we explore the link between prayer and forgiveness as we look at the Lord's prayer and the context in which it was given.

Practicing the Disciplines
Each of the studies focuses on a different spiritual discipline that takes us deeper into the topic.

1. *Scripture study:* we begin with an inductive study that reveals

what the Bible has to say about the topic.

2. *Confession:* we look at ourselves in light of Scripture, taking time in the midst of Bible study for silent reflection and repentance.

3. *Community:* we move to interaction with others around a passage or an exercise, asking for guidance and encouragement as we seek God.

4. *Silence:* again we come before Scripture, but this time seeking not to analyze but to hear God's voice and guidance for us.

5. *Obedience:* in light of Scripture's teaching we make commitments to change.

6. *Prayer:* we take time to seek God weaving prayer through our encounter with Scripture.

These sessions are designed to be completed in 45 minutes to an hour in a group or 30 minutes in personal study. However, feel free to follow the leading of the Holy Spirit and spend as long is needed on each study.

Every session has several components.

Turning Toward God. Discussion or reflection questions and exercises to draw us into the topic at hand.

Receiving God's Word. A Bible study with application and spiritual exercises.

Now or Later. Ideas that can be used at the end of the study as a time of quiet for a group or individual. Or these ideas can be used between studies in quiet times.

The components of this guide can help us meet God with both our minds and hearts. May they also encourage you to forgive others as God has forgiven you.

1

THE CONSEQUENCES OF SIN

....

Practicing the Discipline of Scripture Study

In the video *Burden of Proof* a husband finds a suicide note that says merely, "Can you forgive me?" As the story unfolds, we discover that the wife committed suicide because she couldn't bear the humiliation of having her husband find out that she had committed adultery with a brother-in-law.

Many of us live with skeletons in our closets. However, hiding our sins from God is not an option. David engineered the death of Uriah in order to hide his adultery with Uriah's wife, Bathsheba. It didn't work. In this story we see how God confronts sin and deals with it. We also see a model of a positive way to respond when we are confronted with our own moral failures.

 TURNING TOWARD GOD   *When have you experienced the consequences of a sin you committed?

*How did it affect your relationship with God?

*What do you hope to get out of this series of studies on forgiveness?

The Discipline of Scripture Study

God's Word is one of our greatest resources for knowing him and drawing close to him. What follows is an inductive Bible study that will help you draw out the truths of Scripture for yourself through three types of questions: observation (to gather the facts), interpretation (to discern the meaning) and application (to relate the truths of Scripture to our lives).

 RECEIVING GOD'S WORD 1. Read 2 Samuel 12:1-14. How does Nathan initiate his confrontation with David (vv. 1-4)?

2. David takes the bait and pronounces judgment against the rich man in the parable (vv. 5-6). Why begin with a parable instead of just beginning with a direct statement of the sin?

3. What are common ways that people respond when confronted with something they have done wrong?

How do you respond when someone confronts you with something you have done wrong?

4. In verses 7-9 Nathan brings a direct charge. What are the details of David's offense?

5. God sent Nathan to confront David with his hidden sin. Like David, we all try to cover up things we have done wrong. How has God confronted you?

6. Drawn in by a parable, then exposed and confronted, David makes no attempt to excuse or justify his behavior (v. 13). What are common ways that we attempt to excuse or justify our offenses and moral failures?

7. Nathan assures David that his sin has been taken away, yet he still names consequences. What are they (vv. 10, 13-14)?

8. What are some of the consequences you have experienced from choosing to do what you knew was wrong?

9. Read 2 Samuel 12:15-25. David seeks to change God's mind

through fasting and prayer. Yet when he learns of the child's death, David gives up his grieving and fasting. Why?

How does David's behavior provide a model for us?

10. God consoles David and Bathsheba through the birth of Solomon (v. 24). How is Nathan's role of bringing a name for the child, *Jedidiah,* meaning "loved by the LORD," a continuation of his role at the beginning of this story?

11. What do you learn from this passage about the consequences of sin and the ways God brings judgment and forgiveness?

In Psalm 139 David invites God to search his heart and to see if there are in sinful ways in his heart. As you begin this study on forgiveness, follow David's example and invite God to bring to the surface sins that need to be confessed. As you invite God to search your heart, you can be confident of his gracious response.

NOW OR LATER   Those who are seeking freedom from addictions find that facing covered-up sins from the past is absolutely essential. The fourth step of recovering from addiction in the Twelve Step program is to make a moral inventory. Why not do that in your journal as you begin this study of the spiritual discipline of forgiveness?

2

TURNING TO GOD WITH OUR SIN

···

Practicing the Discipline of Confession

When I was about seven years old, I intentionally disobeyed my father. I got away with my misdeed without being discovered. But I was overwhelmed with a burning sense of guilt.

When I couldn't stand it any longer, I got my father's belt out of the closet and took it to him at the breakfast table. I laid it beside his plate, told him what I had done and said I was ready to take the consequences. He asked me a few questions about my misdeed and nodded disapprovingly. For several minutes I was on the carpet and under the penetrating stare of discerning eyes. Restrictions were applied and privileges withdrawn. And then, instead of getting the belt, I got a hug. The burning guilt I felt inside was replaced with a grateful warmth.

God likes it when we come to him with a burning conscience. David knows that while God may be the judge of our sin, he is also the only place to which we can turn with our sin.

 TURNING TOWARD GOD   *One of the reasons that we hesitate to confess our moral failures is because we fear the consequences. What consequences do you fear in having your transgressions and failures exposed?

*What differences has confessing to God made in your life?

The Discipline of Confession

God calls us to confess our sin to him and to one another. Confession is an opportunity to ask for God's help and mercy. Interacting with this Scripture and the voice of the psalmist will help you open your heart to God. Along the way you'll have some opportunities to confess your own sin. You may want to do this verbally, silently or in writing. Follow God's leading.

 RECEIVING GOD'S WORD   1. Read Psalm 51. What are the consequences of sin that David is experiencing that perhaps motivated him to write this confession?

2. Reread this passage silently. As you read, take time to reflect and pray, confessing your sin to God.

3. Appealing to God's mercy, David asks God to *blot, wash* and

cleanse him from his sin (vv. 1-2). From your own experience what does forgiveness feel like?

4. In this classic psalm of confession, David doesn't ask to be forgiven for his sin, he asked to be *cleansed* (vv. 1, 2, 7). What does this reveal about David's understanding of God?

5. How does David's reference to a sinful birth (v. 5) address the temptation to justify sin by the excuse of good intentions or of momentary impulse?

6. Accountability, responsibility and humility are essential ingredients of a cleansing confession. How does David's confession display these (vv. 3-6)?

7. In light of David's prayer, pray again for yourself, boldly asking to be cleansed from your sin.

8. Look at verses 9-11. Sin pollutes our hearts and creates a distance between ourselves and God. How does David hope that his confession will address these problems?

Describe your own sense of what renewed intimacy with God is like after a cleansing confession.

9. We often fear that if we admit our wrong doing we will be disqualified and unworthy to continue in our responsibilities. Contrast this with David's expectation in verses 13-17.

10. David makes two very different references to sacrifice in verses 16-19. How are the inward sacrifices of a broken and contrite heart and those of burnt offerings both pleasing to God when offered in the appropriate way?

11. David begins with a guilty conscience and ends with a cleansed heart. What were the steps he went through in his transition from guilt to grace?

Take some time now to silently go through those steps and apply them to your heart.

Pray that God will allow you to experience the fruits of confession, the ability to receive God's forgiveness and release from any lingering sense of guilt.

NOW OR LATER   Sometimes God confronts our sin by sending a prophet like Nathan. Sometimes our inward moral compass, which we call a conscience, confronts us. When we face our sin and bring it to God, a great weight of moral failure is lifted and our whole life is renewed. However, sometimes when we confess, it seems that we still feel the weight of our sin. Have you ever confessed a sin and still felt badly about it?

Ask God to give you the experience of being washed. Sit before him and allow him to wash your heart; picture him gently pouring water over your heart and wiping it clean with a cloth.

3

GUIDELINES FOR FORGIVING OTHERS

....

Practicing the Discipline of Community

Sometimes I put on a fire hat and walk around the ministry offices of our church. The sight of it produces wry smiles and knowing nods. It seems like every week there are relational fires to put out, and it is part of my responsibility to help sort things out.

One of the reasons that I can help others sort out conflicts is because I have had a good share of them myself. While painful to experience, I am not surprised by conflict; it is to be expected. It's part of the human experience and the Christian experience. What is unique about conflicts in the Christian community is how we resolve them. Instead of cold shoulders or organized power plays, Christians are to live in the constant experience of forgiving and being forgiven.

The Discipline of Community
God has given us other people in the body of Christ for support and encouragement, as well as enjoyment. As we learn about Christ from Scripture and from each other, we are made complete. For the

following exercises and Scripture study, you need to work with one or two other people or a small group. Ask someone you trust to work through this material with you. (This could include a spouse, but it would be good to include a friend as well.)

> **TURNING TOWARD GOD**   *Compassion literally means "feeling with" or "shared emotions." The word *compassion* is used to describe the act of "feeling with" someone who is hurting. Make a list of significant hurts in your past that might equip you to have compassion with someone in pain.

Discuss your list with your partner. You can share the details of the list or simply talk about patterns that you noticed as you made it.

*Those who are best at showing compassion to others are also good at receiving it. Who has demonstrated compassion to you and how did you receive it?

*God wants Christians to have compassion for others in pain. How do you respond when someone tells you that you have hurt them?

*Those who are hurting are all around us. List several ways that people in your church or community are experiencing pain. How could you "feel with them" and "share their emotions"?

 RECEIVING GOD'S WORD   1. Read Matthew 18:15-20. According to Jesus, what are the steps for dealing with someone who sins against you (vv. 15-17)?

2. Jesus says, "If a brother sins against you" (v. 15). What sort of actions qualify as a sin against another person?

3. How do you generally respond when someone "sins against you"?

4. Many conflicts among Christians are never satisfactorily handled because we either say nothing or talk to other people rather than going directly to our offender. Why do we have such a problem with going directly to another person to tell them we have been hurt by them?

5. The second step in Christian confrontation is to take one or two other people if the first step didn't produce resolution and reconciliation. What happens if we skip step one and go directly to step two?

What happens if step one doesn't work and we don't go on to step two?

6. Jesus takes reconciliation very seriously. What recourse does he provide if someone refuses to listen after steps one and two (vv. 17-19)?

7. What would it be like to be in a community in which hurts and grievances weren't buried, overlooked or ignored?

What can you do to bring that about?

8. Grace extended to another is indicator of our reception of God's grace toward us. What do your responses to others who have hurt you show about your experience of God's grace?

9. How can the natural flow of conflict and resolution within a Christian community be a means of spiritual growth?

Pray that God will give you the courage to confront those who have sinned against you and the heartfelt grace to forgive.

NOW OR LATER   Make a list of people you need to speak to about hurts and offenses.

Next consider whether you have a condemning heart toward them or one of grace and reconciliation.

Make a commitment to pray through your pain and anger until you can be genuinely forgiving.

Think through a time and a place when you can talk to them and the manner in which you will communicate your grievances.

4

RECEIVING GOD'S FORGIVENESS

·······························

Practicing the Discipline of Silence

God is always speaking, but we aren't always listening. Our attempts to have meaningful conversations with God may be blocked by a number of factors. The commotion we create by our actions and by our thoughts makes discerning the voice and presence of God difficult. Inner barriers also make it difficult for us to hear God. We have a sense of guilt, shame or embarrassment and are afraid to hear from God. Finally, like static on the radio, anger and bitterness keep an underlying spiritual noise in our hearts that drowns out the Word. This study is about quieting the noisemakers, receiving God's forgiveness for our failings and learning to listen to God.

The Discipline of Silence

For many of us the disciplines of silence and meditation are the most difficult to pursue. We want to complete a task—read a book of the Bible or pray through a list of needs. Sometimes, however, God wants us to simply come before him and wait to hear his voice. The exercises below are best done in quiet, whether you are in a room with others in your small group or alone. After you complete all the questions on your own, you may discuss them with a group.

TURNING TOWARD GOD *When you get quiet, what do you hear inside your heart and head? Pause for awhile and listen. Write down all that you feel compelled to do. Make a list and then give it over to the Lord.

Go see Ruth — Tom - Internet
Marjorie Ely
Write note
Randy Cuthbert
Birthday mail

*Consider: there is a difference between a dead silence and a full silence. When do you experience a full silence? What do you enjoy about it?

*When do you experience a dead silence? What is it like?

RECEIVING GOD'S WORD 1. Read the following passages through several times.

8 All of you, live in harmony with one another; be sympa-
thetic, love as brothers, be compassionate and humble. 9 Do not repay
evil with evil or insult with insult, but with blessing, because to this
you were called so that you may inherit a blessing. (1 Peter 3:8-9)

13 Bear with each other and forgive whatever grievances you may have
against one another. Forgive as the Lord forgave you. 14 And over all

these virtues put on love, which binds them all together in perfect unity.

[15]Let the peace of Christ rule in your hearts, since as members of one body you were called to peace. And be thankful. [16]Let the word of Christ dwell in you richly as you teach and admonish one another with all wisdom, and as you sing psalms, hymns and spiritual songs with gratitude in your hearts to God. [17]And whatever you do, whether in word or deed, do it all in the name of the Lord Jesus, giving thanks to God the Father through him. (Colossians 3:13-17)

2. Pray for God to guide you to the verses that he wants to show you.

3. Read the passages again slowly.

4. Focus on the passage that most strongly pulls you in. What words or phrases stand out to you? Why?

5. How do these words address the needs in your life?

6. What message does God have for you today?

7. One of the sources of noise in our hearts is a guilty conscience barking at us like a dog on a chain. Ask God to pick up the dog and extend it the quieting comfort of his forgiving grace. As the dog settles down and nestles in the arms of God, relax and enjoy the refreshing rest of knowing that God's grace means that everything is really going to be alright.

What did you experience in your time of reflection?

Pray that God will give you the courage and strength to allow the peace of Christ to dwell in your heart throughout the next week.

NOW OR LATER   Set aside at least fifteen minutes each day this week and practice getting quiet. Write down all the concerns that come to you for the day and give them over to the Lord. After you have unloaded your heart, sit quietly and enjoy a sense of quiet communion with God.

Jill Clough,
Jordan
Sharon

5

WHEN YOU DON'T WANT TO FORGIVE

·······································

Practicing the Discipline of Obedience

There is a member of my extended family that I find very difficult to forgive. The incident that inflicted pain took place more than thirty years ago. My anger toward him is not a constant obsession. But from time to time when I feel the effects of the old scars, I want to become indignant.

Actually I have forgiven him, over and over and over again. I know it is what the Lord wants me to do, and it is what I want to do as well. I am not into holding grudges. Even so, every time I do feel the twinge of anger and choose to forgive, it is an act of obedience.

Forgiveness is a spiritual discipline. That means it is an exercise of the heart, a cultivated desire that comes from the practice of habitual obedience to the requirements of God.

 TURNING TOWARD GOD Consider how you feel toward those who have hurt you. If you find any desires for revenge toward those who have hurt you, bring those desires to the Lord and tell him that you will trust him to bring you justice and meet your needs. Make notes about how this affects you. You may discover a range of feelings from frustration to relief. Make a note of those feelings.

The Discipline of Obedience

God has called us to follow him. Sometimes we deliberately turn away from what we know he wants for us. At other times we wander from him on a gently meandering path. Both are acts of sin that put us out of God's reach. Obedience brings us close to God again. This Bible study and the application questions will help you to discover where you need to turn back toward God.

RECEIVING GOD'S WORD   **1.** Read 1 Samuel 24. This is a dramatic and amusing story of an encounter between Saul and David. Looking at the basic movements in the passage (vv. 1-4, 5-7, 8-15, 16-21 and 22), what background music would you use for each part of the story?

2. Look at verses 1-2. Saul is back from fighting the Philistines. With an army of three thousand he begins a search for David for the purpose of removing him as a threat to his throne and family dynasty. What would David's possible responses be to knowing that an entire army was pursing him?

3. What responses do you have when you know that someone is out to hurt you?

4. According to verses 3-4, David has the opportunity to end Saul's threat to his life and remove him as an obstacle to the divinely promised throne of Israel. What reasons would he have for killing Saul?

How might this dangerous opportunity be seen as humorous?

5. David is conscience-stricken for cutting off a piece of Saul's robe (vv. 5-7). What was wrong with merely cutting off a piece of Saul's robe instead of killing him?

What does David's concern over this action reveal about his character?

6. David listens to his conscience and acts with a sense of spiritual obedience. What sort of social and political dynamics might have been unleashed in Israel if David had taken this opportunity to defend himself and seize the throne?

7. Reflect on your life history. Can you discern any negative consequences you might have avoided because you acted in spiritual obedience as opposed to seizing a convenient opportunity? Or conversely, can you identify negative consequences you did experience because you did something that you knew was wrong? Explain.

8. What does David want Saul to know about his intentions (vv. 8-11)?

9. What reasons does David give to explain why he didn't seize the opportunity to kill Saul (vv. 12-15)?

10. How might David's example be a help to you when you face hostility or misunderstanding?

11. What does Saul's response in verses 16-21 indicate about his perception of David?

12. David and Saul go their separate ways (v. 22). While there was no reconciliation, what do both David and Saul gain from the encounter?

13. What have you learned about the process of forgiveness from this passage?

Although the king was a sinner, David honored him as king and refused to take hostile actions. Conclude this study by praying for God's grace on your spiritual and political leaders.

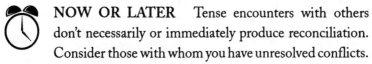 **NOW OR LATER**   Tense encounters with others don't necessarily or immediately produce reconciliation. Consider those with whom you have unresolved conflicts. Plan what you can do this week to open doors for ongoing process of communication.

6

KEEPING PERSPECTIVE

....

Practicing the Discipline
of Prayer

While I am struggling with a sense of guilt toward Darlene, I am
confident that she will forgive me. All I have to do is ask. Not only
will that remove that pang of conscience every time I see her, but I
will again be able to enjoy being with her.

This is the wonder of forgiveness—whether it is forgiveness from
God or from others that we need. Once forgiveness has been asked
for and extended, the pleasure of friendship and the experience of
love is restored.

Guilt does terrible things to people. It hardens personal barriers
into solid concrete walls. On the other hand, forgiveness does
wonderful things to people. It softens personal barriers so that they
dissolve.

Guilt makes life a splash of burning colors in a patchwork of
chaos. Forgiveness weaves all the conflicts and patches of life into
a quilt with a divine pattern of beauty and symmetry.

As we conclude this study on forgiveness, we come to the final
act that empowers forgiveness: prayer.

The Discipline of Prayer

Prayer draws us close to God. It is an opportunity to give him our concerns and to listen for his voice. In prayer we may not always feel that we have connected with God, but as we remain faithful in seeking him, we will experience the riches of companionship with God. Our desire for and understanding of prayer grows as we study Scripture.

TURNING TOWARD GOD   *At the root of anxiety is a knowledge that life is beyond our control and a fear that it may be out of control. At the root of prayer is a knowledge life is beyond our control but well within the power of God. Make a list of things you are anxious about and choose to prayerfully relinquish them to God. *I pray that.*

Desks get to WA OK.
Tom gets here before dinnertime.
Jim continues well
Matthew has surgery OK.

*What have you learned though these studies about forgiveness as a discipline to be exercised, a disposition to be cultivated and a skill to be practiced?

RECEIVING GOD'S WORD   1. Read Matthew 6:1-15. Jesus teaches about two acts of righteousness in the Jewish religion: giving to the needy (vv. 2-4) and prayer (vv. 5-15). What hypocrisy is common to both acts of righteousness?

2. In every judgment that Jesus makes there is an opportunity for grace. As you look over Jesus' instructions for prayer, what clues do you get regarding the remedy for hypocrisy?

3. How do you feel about going without recognition for the things you do for God and others?

4. Prayer is the central act of righteousness (vv. 5-15). In addition to praying in secret, Jesus adds two additional correctives, brevity and forgiveness. How are they reflected in the model prayer he provides?

5. The Lord's Prayer is one of the most familiar of all Jesus' teaching. Many of us pray it at least weekly in a worship service. Read verses 9-13 aloud and then silently in an attitude of prayer.

How does Jesus' prayer provide a corrective to the way you live and pray?

6. Jesus makes our experience of divine forgiveness dependent on our forgiveness of others (vv. 11, 14-15). How does this make you feel?

7. How does an unforgiving heart impact our experience of God's presence in prayer?

8. If we made a commitment to a lifestyle of forgiveness, how often in a day or week do you think you might have to exercise forgiveness?

9. How do you think a lifestyle of forgiveness would affect you?

How do you think it would affect your family?

How about your colleagues?

What about the members of your church?

Ask God to continue to grow your understanding of what it means to forgive. Ask him to teach you how to pray for forgiveness.

NOW OR LATER   Keep a written record this week of every time you feel offended. Don't show this to anyone but God. At the end of each day pull out the list and go over it with God. Tell him why you were offended and how the offense made you feel. Then extend forgiveness merely because the Lord has forgiven you. At the end of the week review your list, note which offenses you are still struggling with and which you really have been able to turn over to God. Once you have done this, burn your list in a safe place as an offering to God.

Guidelines for Leaders

My grace is sufficient for you. (2 Corinthians 12:9)

If leading a small group is something new for you, don't worry. These sessions are designed to be led easily. As a matter of fact, the flow of questions in the Bible study portions through the passage from observation to interpretation to application is so natural that you may feel that the studies lead themselves.

You don't need to be an expert on the Bible or a trained teacher to lead a small group discussion. The idea behind these sessions is that the leader guides group members to discover for themselves what the Bible has to say and to listen for God's guidance. This method of learning will allow group members to remember much more of what is said than a lecture would.

This study guide is flexible. You can use it with a variety of groups— student, professional, neighborhood or church groups. Each study takes forty-five to sixty minutes in a group setting.

There are some important facts to know about group dynamics and encouraging discussion. The suggestions listed below should enable you to effectively and enjoyably fulfill your role as leader.

Preparing for the Study

1. Ask God to help you understand and apply the passage in your own life. Unless this happens, you will not be prepared to lead others. Pray too for the various members of the group. Ask God to open your hearts to the message of his Word and motivate you to action.

2. Read the introduction to the entire guide to get an overview of the issues which will be explored.

3. As you begin each study, read and reread the assigned Bible passage to familiarize yourself with it.

4. This study guide is based on the New International Version of the Bible. It will help you and the group if you use this translation as the basis for your study and discussion.

5. Carefully work through each question in the study. Spend time in meditation and reflection as you consider how to respond.

6. Write your thoughts and responses in the space provided in the study guide. This will help you to express your understanding of the passage clearly.

7. It might help to have a Bible dictionary handy. Use it to look up any unfamiliar words, names or places. (For additional help on how to study a passage, see chapter five of *Leading Bible Discussions,* InterVarsity Press.)

8. Consider how you need to apply the Scripture to your life. Remember that the group will follow your lead in responding to the studies. They will not go any deeper than you do.

Leading the Study

1. Begin the study on time. Open with prayer, asking God to help the group to understand and apply the passage.

2. Be sure that everyone in your group has a study guide. There are some questions and activities they will need to work through on their own—either beforehand or during the study session.

3. The flow of each study varies a bit. Many of the studies have time for silent reflection as well as for group discussion. Think through how you will lead the groups through the times of silence, and read through the notes for guidance. It can be very powerful to have times of silence in the midst of a group session. Session four focuses on silence particularly and calls for an extended time apart. Then you can come together and share your experiences.

4. At the beginning of your first time together, explain that these studies are meant to be discussions, not lectures. Encourage the members of the group to participate. However, do not put pressure on those who may be hesitant to speak during the first few sessions. You may want to suggest

the following guidelines to your group.

☐ Stick to the topic being discussed.

☐ Your responses should be based on the verses which are the focus of the discussion and not on outside authorities such as commentaries or speakers.

☐ These studies focus on a particular passage of Scripture. Only rarely should you refer to other portions of the Bible. This allows for everyone to participate on equal ground and for in-depth study.

☐ Anything said in the group is considered confidential and will not be discussed outside the group unless specific permission is given to do so.

☐ Provide time for each person present to talk if he or she feels comfortable doing so.

☐ Listen attentively to each other and learn from one another.

☐ Pray for each other.

5. Have a group member read the introduction at the beginning of the discussion.

6. Every session begins with the "Turning Toward God" section. The questions or activities are meant to be used before the passage is read. These questions introduce the theme of the study and encourage group members to begin to open up. Encourage as many members as possible to participate, and be ready to get the discussion going with your own response.

7. Either prior to or right after "Turning Toward God," you will see a definition of the specific discipline the session focuses on. Have someone read that explanation.

8. Have one or more group member(s) read aloud the passage to be studied.

9. As you ask the questions under "Receiving God's Word," keep in mind that they are designed to be used just as they are written. You may simply read them aloud. Or you may prefer to express them in your own words.

There may be times when it is appropriate to deviate from the study guide. For example, a question may have already been answered. If so, move on to the next question. Or someone may raise an important question not covered in the guide. Take time to discuss it, but try to keep the group from going off on tangents.

10. Avoid answering your own questions. If necessary, repeat or rephrase them until they are clearly understood. Or point out something you read in the leader's notes to clarify the context or meaning. An eager group quickly becomes passive and silent if they think the leader will do most of the talking.

11. Don't be afraid of silence in response to the discussion questions. People may need time to think about the question before formulating their answers.

12. Don't be content with just one answer. Ask, "What do the rest of you think?" or "Anything else?" until several people have given answers to the question.

13. Acknowledge all contributions. Try to be affirming whenever possible. Never reject an answer. If it is clearly off-base, ask, "Which verse led you to that conclusion?" or again, "What do the rest of you think?"

14. Don't expect every answer to be addressed to you, even though this will probably happen at first. As group members become more at ease, they will begin to truly interact with each other. This is one sign of healthy discussion.

15. Don't be afraid of controversy. It can be very stimulating. If you don't resolve an issue completely, don't be frustrated. Move on and keep it in mind for later. A subsequent study may solve the problem.

16. Periodically summarize what the group has said about the passage. This helps to draw together the various ideas mentioned and gives continuity to the study. But don't preach.

17. At the end of the Bible discussion you may want to allow group members a time of quiet to work on an idea under "Now or Later." Then discuss what you experienced. Or you may want to encourage group members to work on these ideas between meetings. Give an opportunity during the session to allow people to talk about what they are learning.

18. Conclude your time together with conversational prayer, adapting the prayer suggestion at the end of the study to your group. Ask for God's help in following through on the commitments you've made.

19. End on time.

Many more suggestions and helps are found in *Small Group Leader's Handbook* and *The Big Book on Small Groups* (both from InterVarsity Press). Reading through one of these books would be worth your time.

Study Notes

Study 1. The Consequences of Sin. 2 Samuel 12:1-25.
Purpose: To learn to take responsibility for our sin and face the consequences of sin as the necessary steps for receiving God's forgiveness.
Turning Toward God. The first question may cause such discomfort that groups members are hesitant to answer. Perhaps you can free people by telling them they don't have to say what sin they committed, just something of the consequences.

The final question in this section is important. Don't skip over it. It calls your entire group to a sense of purpose for the next six meetings. Why not have everyone actually write down a couple of goals now with a date beside it? Then when you have worked through the series, you can come back to your written goals to see how well your expectations matched the outcome.
The Discipline of Scripture Study. Every study in this guide is written using the inductive study pattern of observation, interpretation and application. As the leader, you might find it helpful to notice this pattern as you prepare to lead each study.
Question 3. Don't hurry over this question. Encourage people to dig into their own experience with others and look at their own patterns as well.
Question 6. Ask this question with a gracious sense of probing. Surely this is one of the reasons that David was described as a man after God's own heart. Like all of us, he was a sinner. However, unlike many of us, when confronted with sin he makes no excuse or attempt to justify himself.

Any attempt to explain away sin or excuse it is an attempt to deny our responsibility and guilt. It is important to keep in mind that there is a great difference between forgiving and excusing. God never excuses our sin. He forgives it.

Question 7. We are tempted to think that forgiveness means that there will be no consequences. This passage demonstrates that God works differently. In the New Testament we learn that God forgives our sins, but the eternal consequences of our sins have fallen on Jesus as he died on the cross. However, as we live out our salvation, we must still, in this life, experience the earthly consequences of sin as they affect others and ourselves.

Question 9. David demonstrates his faith, in prayer, and seeks God's help for his child with great intensity. However, he also knows that God is not bound to answer our prayers in the way we want him to. David is both able to seek God and accept the answers that God gives.

Question 10. This answer may not be immediately obvious. Nathan's role in pronouncing judgment and bringing consolation are both expressions of the loving presence and ruling hand of God in the lives of his people.

Question 11. Principles of the consequences of sin and of forgiveness might include: God knows all our actions. God holds us morally responsible for all our actions. Everybody can and does commit sin. We can be morally blind. Confrontation may be necessary to uncover sin. We need to accept moral responsibility. Our sin has consequences that affect our families and friends. God is willing to forgive. God comforts us even as we are experiencing the consequences of our sin.

Now or Later. Consider planning time for group members to do the moral inventory during the meeting. Perhaps people could go off into other parts of the room to work on it. Or if you prefer and time requires it, encourage people to set aside a time and a place during the week. Check back on progress next week.

Study 2. Turning to God with Our Sin. Psalm 51.

Purpose: To explore the feelings of shame that accompany sin and to consider the way in which God not only forgives sin but addresses our feelings as well.

Turning Toward God. This exercise sets up the study of Psalm 51. Not only are there external consequences to sinning, there are internal consequences as well. Long after the external consequences have come and gone, the internal consequences may continue.

Concerning the feared consequences of sin, people may have to think about this for a while, be sure to give them adequate time.

The Discipline of Confession. Guilt and shame go hand in hand. Guilt is our legal culpability for breaking the law, shame is the bad feeling we have about our guilt. Both guilt and shame tend to drive us into hiding, creating social and emotional isolation. Confession directly confronts the shame that we feel and rescues us from the darkness in which we may be trapped.

Question 2. Allow five to ten minutes of silence for prayer and reflection. You may want to bring the group back together by singing a praise song like "Create in Me a Clean Heart" or playing a song from a CD.

Questions 3-4. These questions are intended to tie into question 1, bringing out the internal experience of the consequences of sin. David writes wonderfully about the need to feel clean after the effects of sin.

Question 5. David's reference to being guilty from birth could be taken as an attempt to place the blame on his inborn nature. "I couldn't help it, this is the way I was born to be." In contrast, he is saying that his sinning is not a new development or a passing phase in his life. In essence, he is saying, "I am a sinner from way back when."

Question 6. As we saw in the last study, when confronted with his sin David makes no attempt to excuse or explain away his responsibility. Further, he displays a deep personal knowledge that in all he does, he is accountable to God. In essence, in verses 3-6 he says, "I deserve the judgments that you have made about me."

Question 7. If you are leading a group, you might want to make this a time of group prayer, asking God for cleansing for yourselves and for one another. The prayer concerns need not be specific.

Question 8. Guilt and shame drive us from the presence of God. Consider, for example, how Adam and Eve hid in the bushes of the Garden of Eden when God showed up for his afternoon walk. David, in contrast, asks for a continued experience of God's presence.

Question 9. David knows that his sin has not made him worthless for the rest of his life. Instead he knows that the experience of God's grace puts him in a position to extend that grace to others. You will probably get a lively discussion if you invite members of your group to think about their attitude toward fallen Christian leaders in light of these verses.

Question 10. One of the references to sacrifice is ceremonial, the offering of burnt offerings is external. The other is internal, that of a broken spirit and a contrite heart.

Question 11. Allow a few minutes of silence for people to reflect on the second part of this question, and then move into a time of prayer.

Now or Later. This exercise of allowing God to wash the heart can be very powerful. Lead your group through this if you can do so comfortably. (Not everyone feels comfortable praying with the imagination.)

Study 3. Guidelines for Forgiving Others. Matthew 18:15-20.

Purpose: To explore the process of confrontation and forgiveness necessary for living in a godly way within the community of Christ's church.

Turning to God. First responses to conflict or inflected relational pains include a *fight* or *flight*. Either we respond aggressively and want to *fight* it out or we turn from the conflict and flee. The first response, for a Christian, should be to go to God. This exercise provides a way for your group to do just that. Give your group members time to think about and perhaps write down in a prayer how they feel after being hurt by someone.

Having done this, allow your group members to think about how God feels toward them in response to their pains. We often do not take the time to be with God in a way that we can experience God's compassion toward us.

General note. These questions explore the heart of relational reconciliation. Taking these verses seriously and applying them will cut to the heart of social conflicts and provide a means of resolution. The real problem we have is finding the courage to do what Jesus says.

Question 2. There is no official list of "sins against another." However, commandments 5-10 from Exodus 20 contain the heart of all social sins.

Question 8. Until we have internally experienced the forgiveness of God, we won't genuinely be able to give that grace to others.

Now or Later. This section will help you work through the process of forgiveness. It would be best to begin this in a group so you can encourage each other. Before you work through these questions, it might be best to take a break from study and give five or ten minutes for silent reflection. Then discuss how you might encourage each other to seek out those with whom reconciliation needs to take place.

Study 4. Receiving God's Forgiveness. 1 Peter 3:8-9; Colossians 3:13-17.
Purpose: To allow time to reflect on the inner personal dynamics of care and community that nurture an environment of forgiveness.
Turning to God. Read the paragraph on the "Discipline of Silence" to the group. Give about five minutes for people to make the list described in the first question. Then ask them about their experience and discuss the other two questions in this section.

Being silent together in a group is a powerful experience if it is set up well. In my experience there is often a rich sense of God's presence. Once a group moves into silence, it often feels like an abrupt intrusion when you have to move on to discussion.

On the other hand, spending time in silence, both as a group and personally, can be very threatening. As the leader, you need to set up this time. You need to both invite the group to be silent and then invite them to enjoy the silence.

Receiving God's Word. Once you have gone through the introductory material, you will be in a position to enjoy the rest of the study. Invite group members to move to a quiet spot in the place where you meet, if possible, in order to do this study. (If the weather permits, this might be a good time for an outdoor study.)

Before you break up, you might read the passages aloud. After you spend time working through the passages alone, get back together and talk about what happened in their silent reflection.

A word of caution, some people will love the silent time of study, some people may not like it all! As a leader, it is your role to help your group members understand that both responses are "normal" and to be expected. However they respond, each group member will still have profitable insights to offer.

Study 5. When You Don't Want to Forgive. 1 Samuel 24.

Purpose: To explore the challenges and beneficial results that come from living a life of forgiveness.

Turning Toward God. Allow group members silent time to work through this material. Encourage people to do some journaling or at least jot down notes about things that come to mind. After your group has had time to do some personal work, you might want to lead in prayer. As you pray, invite people to silently take their concerns before the Lord and lay them at his feet. After the prayer time, allow several minutes for discussion of what happened when they prayed and how they feel about it.

Question 1. This is an unusual question. However, it should allow you to enter into the humor and drama of this passage in a fresh way. Have fun with it as you move into the story and its meaning.

Question 2. Few of us will ever find an army chasing us. But we all know what it is like to be disliked and displaced. Look first at David's possible emotional responses and then encourage your group to identify with him.

Question 4. Not only was David a fugitive from Saul who was trying to kill him, he also had a promise from God that the throne would be given to him. He could have chosen to see this opportunity as a gift from God to take what was going to be rightfully his.

Question 5. David's action is a clever means of making his presence known. It is, however, an act of aggression against the anointed king of Israel. This act violates David's commitment to honor the king.

Question 6. In the history of Israel, Jehu was anointed by a prophet to be given the throne after it was to be taken away from Ahab and Jezebel. Jehu initiated a coup and killed both Ahab and Jezebel. His act unleashed a bloodbath of violence that swept the nation. You can read about it in 2 Kings 9—10. In contrast, although David is promised the throne, he does not take this as a divine right for a coup. The result was that, when he did receive the throne after the death of Saul in battle, he was able to unite the entire nation under his rule and establish a peace that lasted through his reign and that of his son Solomon.

Questions 8-10. David is obedient to God and forgiving toward Saul, but he is not a silent martyr. He wants Saul to know that his actions prove that he is not out to hurt the king. In doing this David sets a model worth following. It is important to speak up for ourselves and make the intentions of our hearts known in the midst of interpersonal conflict.

Question 11. Saul is a fearful person. He appears to understand and respond to David's action and his appeal. Yet he will continue in the immediate future to feel threatened by David and suspicious of his intentions. He is fearful of David's abilities, his standing with the people of the nation, and of David's relationship with God.

Question 12. Not all confrontation produces reconciliation. Yet confrontation and clear communication are important. Both men spoke their hearts to each other and this provides an opportunity to live and relate with integrity. Use this question to explore the importance of integrity and communication that may or may not lead to reconciliation.

Now or Later. This exercise builds on question 10 in this study. It would provide a good closing for your group. Give group members time to think about who they need to talk to. It might be good to allow some time for reflection and jotting of notes. As appropriate, encourage people to share what they have written about their plans for communication with people they have conflict with.

Study 6. Keeping Perspective. Matthew 6:1-15.

Purpose: To explore the importance of prayer in living a life of forgiveness.

Turning Toward God. Allow people time to make a list of anxieties. After they have done so, lead the group in a leisurely time of prayer in which you provide encouragement and guidance to give those anxieties to God. After your prayer, take a few minutes to lead in reflection in what it feels like to turn over our anxieties to God.

It would be wise to explore the second question with your group before moving into this final study. Together look back through the guide and summarize the issues and dynamics of forgiveness. Encourage people to talk about what they have learned and how they have been affected.

Questions 1-3. Draw out your group by asking a few probing questions and giving enough time to allow them to consider the power of social approval and how it affects them. Social reality often governs our actions as we perceive how others think and feel about us. In contrast, we may not so easily perceive the attention and affirmation of God. This of course makes it difficult to insure that all our acts of righteousness are for the eyes of God alone. Jesus requires a knowledge of faith that deeply affects our thoughts and actions that go beyond social approval.

As a pastor, I struggle with this. When I find when my actions don't receive the affirmation and appreciation that I desire, my first response is to mutter about it with a sense of indignation, "Nobody really appreciates me . . ." It is only after I've worked my frustration through in prayer that I can let go of that desire for social approval and be satisfied that God knows what I have done.

Question 4. This question encourages reflection on the structure of the Lord's Prayer. We pray this prayer so often and we are so familiar with it that we may fail to see how comprehensive and powerful it is.

Question 5. Have someone read the prayer aloud, thoughtfully. Then allow several minutes of silent prayer and reflection before you ask the question that follows.

Questions 6-7. These questions focus this study on forgiveness, the theme of this guide. All of the dynamics of forgiveness come to bear on the experience and practice of prayer.

Question 8. A central theme in the Lord's teaching on prayer is a predisposition of forgiveness. Forgiveness is to be a "habit of the heart" that comes out of the experience of a forgiven heart. We need to be predisposed to forgive on a daily basis.

Now or Later. This exercise helps us become aware of just how often we are hurt and brush over it. Becoming aware will provide a basis for the right response, giving our hurts to God, rather than the wrong responses of self protection and/or holding grudges.